Introduction

Everybody wants their RE to be inclusive, but how do we make it happen? This book offers answers in key areas. Inclusion is about providing effective learning opportunities for all pupils, irrespective of ability or disability, ethnicity, gender, or religious, social or economic background. It is about valuing pupils as individuals and working to ensure that they achieve the best they can, both academically and personally. Religious education is about helping pupils from all religious or non-religious worldviews to consider, question and take seriously the beliefs and practices of others. This can enable them to understand better the world in which we live by considering issues to do with our shared human experience.

The personal search for identity, meaning and purpose in RE must be inclusive too, so that learners understand themselves and others better. At its heart, therefore, the RE classroom should be an inclusive classroom, catering for the varying needs of all, irrespective of their differences, including their religious or life-stance differences. RE deals with some 'tough issues' for today's world. For some, their religious belief leads them to exclude others' beliefs and practices, regarding their own as God-given and superior. This can manifest itself, for example, in relation to militant evangelism or attitudes towards gender or disability. In a minority of cases it can manifest itself in suicide bombers and terrorism. It is important that the RE classroom provides a safe space in which such issues can be considered.

The ideas and approaches outlined focus on different areas where inclusion (and exclusion) is considered. They exemplify approaches to help towards developing inclusive RE classrooms. It's a short book, but we intend these strategies to point the way to developing practice in your own school: the ideas are easily adaptable for pupils of different abilities and ages.

Lat Blaylock

with thanks to Pamela Draycott for her initial work on this publication.

Contents

RE and inclusion – FAQ

1. What is 'inclusion'? How does it relate to RE?

Inclusion: providing **effective learning opportunities for all pupils** *(irrespective of ability (academic, physical), ethnicity, gender, religious, social or economic background).*

All pupils have an **entitlement** to a **broad and balanced curriculum**. That entitlement includes **RE**, the content of which is selected, drawing on the legal basis for RE in the particular school, and bearing in mind a range of religious (and non-religious) beliefs and life-stances. In order to mediate this content effectively teachers need to select **experiences and opportunities** that meet the **specific learning needs** of **individuals and groups of pupils**.

In England the statutory **inclusion statement**, (see pages 39-46 of the *Non-Statutory National Framework for RE*, QCA 2004, and being incorporated into many locally agreed syllabuses and diocesan guidelines) sets out **three principles** that are essential to developing more inclusive RE:

- **Setting suitable learning challenges**: this means selecting and targeting content and approaches to give every pupil the chance to succeed in their learning and achieve as high a standard as possible. It could mean selecting content from a lower or a higher age group (key stage) in order to meet the needs of particular pupils or groups of pupils.

- **Responding to pupils' diverse learning needs**: this means ensuring high expectations and providing tasks that engage, support and challenge pupils to achieve their best. It means creating an effective learning culture in RE, focused on raising standards. It means considering the different individuals and groups of pupils being taught (bearing in mind gender, ethnicity, etc.) and being aware of the different experiences, interests and strengths that influence the way in which they learn. It means considering different learning styles and approaches and ensuring a variety of tasks and approaches to meet pupils' needs.

- **Overcoming potential barriers to learning and assessment for individuals and groups of pupils**: this means taking action to ensure that individuals or groups of pupils are enabled to participate fully in the curriculum and in assessment practices. This means, for example, taking into account individual education plans (IEPs). In order to provide access it may mean, for example, having taped end-of-unit test questions for pupils with particular reading difficulties and allowing them to answer on tape rather than in writing

2. How do differentiation and personalised learning relate to inclusion? What does this mean for RE?

Differentiation: is meeting the needs of pupils by **selecting appropriate content, tasks** *and* **approaches** *to* **support** *and* **challenge** *their* **learning**.

Personalised learning: is not individualised learning but focuses on meeting the needs of the **individual within group settings and through group interaction**. *The focus is on* **skill development** *to enable learning to take place more effectively and thus raise* **standards** *further.*

To include all pupils, tasks need to be matched to provide adequate support and challenge to enable learning to take place. In RE this means, for example:

- planning for a **range of different learning styles** and on occasion allowing choice of task matched to suit such learning styles, e.g. same content focus with a choice of one of three activities developed with **visual, kinaesthetic** and **auditory** learners in mind;

- taking into account and developing **tasks** that suit **boys and girls approaches to learning**;

- considering how particular ethnic, social, gender or academic groups are achieving, **identifying patterns of underachievement and targeting improvement**;

- developing a **range of differentiation strategies** (outcome, task, resource, support given, etc.) to meet the needs of all pupils;

- developing **skills** (research, analysis, synthesis, etc.) to enable pupils to **see connections, make links** and **apply learning** from one situation to another;

- allowing some **choice of activity and task** to encourage and maintain **interest**, build **self-esteem** and improve **learning motivation**.

3. How can we improve the achievement of special educational needs (SEN) pupils in RE?

We need, for example, to:

- set **tasks** that are **supportive** and **challenging** with clearly **broken down learning stages** that build on each other and offer **variety** to maintain interest;

- give thought to the planning of an appropriate amount of time for pupils to complete tasks;

- provide opportunities whereby pupils **focus** on the **RE learning outcome** rather than focusing solely on literacy development through copying out or reprocessing text;

- plan lessons where there is opportunity to develop the pupils' understanding through **using as many senses as possible**;

- **use** IEPs to guide the necessary **support** for pupils with SEN, **liaising** closely with the SENCO and any learning assistant supporting through the lesson;

- ensure that all **support staff** are clear about the specific RE learning objectives;

- plan for a balance of activities between those that maintain, consolidate, reinforce and generalise skills and also those where pupils are introduced to new knowledge, skills and understanding.

4. How can we raise the achievement of our most able (Gifted and Talented) pupils in RE?

We need, for example, to:

- set tasks which focus on **skill development**, i.e. **tasks** that encourage pupils to **interpret** symbol, metaphor, text or story rather than **recount** what it is or retell the story; use a variety **of open-ended questioning strategies** to engage pupils in thinking at a deeper level: 'Why is this?' rather than 'What is this?';

- use more demanding tasks, questions and sometimes content from key stages beyond the age of the pupil to encourage pupils to **analyse, argue** and **apply** what they are learning;

- set **extension tasks** to deepen or broaden understanding and reflection and not extension tasks that are 'more of the same';

- consider if our more able always need to complete the main classroom task before moving onto the extension task. Is that where they ought to be starting?

- consider the ways in the most able are **grouped**, allowing opportunity to work with others similarly able, to work with older pupils and to support other pupils in their learning.

5. Does including everyone mean accepting any belief/view as being as valid as any other?

Including all means **valuing diversity**, developing **respect for all**, and promoting **tolerance** but it does not mean ignoring real and on occasion very **strongly held differences** in beliefs and values within and across religious belief and practice. Neither does it mean ignoring the **religious exclusivity** that can be a cause of conflict in the world today. RE needs to deal with such **controversial issues** in **open** and **rational ways** and provide pupils with opportunities to, for example, **analyse** different religious points of view, **compare** and **contrast** ideas and **reflect** on and **come to conclusions** about beliefs and practices and their impact for believers in the world today. An inclusive RE classroom takes this into account to support the relevance and applicability of RE learning for today's (and tomorrow's) world. RE is about disagreeing respectfully, which is a key life skill.

6. What can the RE department do?

Some **self-evaluation questions** to ask in relation to **inclusion**:

(Grade as follows: 1 = Outstanding, 2 = Good, 3 = Satisfactory and 4 = Inadequate. Supplement each question with 'How do we know and what do we need to do to target further improvement?')

- How well do we, through our RE **curriculum content** and **planning**, improve the **experiences and opportunities** we offer to *all our pupils*?

- In order to meet the **learning needs** of *all our pupils*, how effective is our **identification of individual and group need**? How effective is our **monitoring** of what individuals and groups achieve, and how do we **modify practice** to **improve standards** further?

- How good are we at targeting the learning needs of *all our pupils* through using **different strategies** to **differentiate learning** – outcome, task, resource, content, amount of time allowed, amount of support given?

- How effective is our **use of levels** in RE (for **task setting** and **assessment purposes**) in raising **expectations** and **improving standards** for *all our pupils*?

7. Where can I find out more?

A first and crucial reference point for RE is the statutory locally agreed syllabus, faith community guidelines, or equivalent (e.g. Religious and Moral Education Guidelines, Scotland (www.ltscotland.org.uk/5to14). Also, any non-statutory guidelines published by local SACREs and/or faith community bodies. The information provided here draws significantly from the following:

Non-statutory National Framework for RE (QCA 2004) and ***Meeting the Needs of the Gifted, Talented and Most Able in RE*** (QCA 2000) – **www.qca.org.uk**.

DFES – standards site www.standards.dfes.gov.uk/giftedandtalented/ and www.standards.dfes.gov.uk/personalisedlearning/

QCA – www.qca.org.uk/inclusion/ which includes information on general inclusion issues, 'Respect for All' and 'Planning, Teaching and Assessing the Curriculum for Pupils with Learning Difficulties'.

RE Today's website has free resources to download on teaching gifted and talented pupils: www.retoday.org.uk/downloads.htm#gt

Meeting the needs of all: teaching to the learning styles of pupils

For the teacher

All pupils need a range of approaches and activities in RE to learn effectively, keep interest and maintain concentration. Providing opportunities for pupils to complete tasks using their preferred learning styles is one way of meeting the needs of a wide group of pupil ability within the secondary classroom.

In 2004 the DfES published a document for subject leaders in secondary schools entitled *Pedagogy and Practice: Teaching and Learning in Secondary Schools, Unit 4: Lesson Design for Inclusion.* The emphasis within this, and in documentation regarding the inclusion of pupils with SEN is that it is crucial to **know your pupils**.

It is also important to liaise with **the Special Educational Needs Co-ordinator (SENCO)** within school, to ensure you have as much information about the learning needs of the pupils as possible and also to ensure that you are aware of where they are in their learning. The assessment data collected on pupils in different subject areas is also important, as pupils may be working at a significantly lower level in literacy, for example, which will be crucial to know when it comes to planning a writing task for pupils in RE. Pupils may be very articulate at explaining the religious beliefs expressed by a visitor but may find it very difficult to record that information.

The guidance on *Lesson Design for Inclusion* (DfES, 2004) notes that every teacher will need to consider, in their planning, the ways in which lessons provide for the full range of learning styles of their pupils.

Bandler and Grinder's theory on sensory preferences is that everyone has a dominant sense that is visual, auditory or kinaesthetic, and that will be the most preferred and also most efficient way of learning.

Key questions to think about

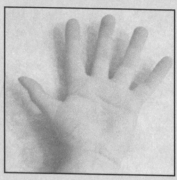

A kinaesthetic learner: Which pupils are able to learn best when they physically move and act out a religious story dramatically? Or when they are able to spend quality time investigating a range of religious artefacts? Who responds with enthusiasm to being able to take part in visits to a place of worship or to re-enact a religious ceremony?

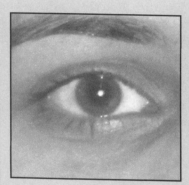

The visual learner: Which pupils enjoy mapping activities or answering questions about religious art? Who's motivated by using contemporary film and video? Which pupils respond well when asked to look at an image and reflect on what life is like for the person in the picture?

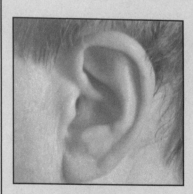

The auditory learner: Which pupils enjoy having the opportunity to use musical instruments to reflect how hearing a religious story has made them feel? Who can respond with imagination after hearing a guided fantasy? Which pupils listen to contemporary religious music and are able to reflect on what it says about belief?

RE today
Services

Planning for an inclusive RE classroom
These are some of the principles that underpin inclusive teaching and learning

All of the pupils are clear what they will be learning in the lesson. Objectives are visible. Pupils know what their group/individual tasks are in the lesson. They also know the criteria to be used to assess whether the learning has been achieved.	**Lesson starters** create links with the prior knowledge, understanding and experiences of pupils. **Plenaries** are used to ask pupils to reflect on what they have learnt in the lesson and to consider how this fits with their learning in the next lesson.	**Pupils are asked to talk about the tasks they are working on,** to check for understanding or gain knowledge of subject matter through discussion with peers. **Pupils are also encouraged to ask questions** in order to help their understanding.
Pupils have personal targets. These could be specific to RE or cross-curricular: using a writing frame to compose a short story or poem, a creative RE response or a learning target from literacy. The pupils need to own the targets: can they discuss their successes in learning for themselves?	**Links are made to pupil learning in other curriculum areas.** Links can also be made to any additional support group that is offered to a pupil and can enable pupils to transfer experiences, knowledge and understanding in different contexts.	**Strategies for active engagement.** This involves pupils working to their preferred learning style. Options for differentiation include pupils choosing their responses to tasks and also choosing to study a topic in RE they are particularly interested in.

How can we plan to include all pupils in RE?

- Inclusive classrooms can be achieved through **careful planning and lesson design**.

- The principles of inclusion within the Strategy are integral to the design of the lesson: **setting suitable learning challenges, responding to pupils' diverse learning needs and overcoming potential barriers to learning and assessment for individuals and groups of pupils**.

- There have to be **clear learning objectives and intended outcomes**. This may imply modification for some pupils. Careful thought must be given to the way tasks are **differentiated**, especially to avoid over reliance on 'outcomes' as the only form of differentiation.

- There needs to be a **range of activities** to support the objectives.

- There needs to be a **clear focus on the pedagogic approaches** used so that those selected meet the needs of all pupils.

- **High expectations need to be set for all pupils.** It is important to know where pupils are in their learning and the next steps. For some pupils these may be small steps of progress. For pupils working at a significantly lower level than their peers, there may need to be a focus on the experiences the pupils are having and on consolidating and maintaining skills already acquired.

- **Classroom organisation** is an important factor in meeting a wide range of pupil need.

- **Targeted additional support** needs to be utilised and staff delivering the support need to be aware of the learning objectives and intended outcomes for supported pupils.

Do all people matter in religion? Four inclusive activities

For the teacher

RE offers pupils opportunities to think about the impact of religious belief on a believer's approach to 'inclusion' and the need to include others. Outlined are four activities which are useful 'ways in' to considering some of the issues surrounding 'inclusion', whilst also looking at how the tasks can be used to include a variety of pupil need within the RE classroom. The four activities can be used with pupils of differing abilities and there are suggestions for differentiation included. The activities draw on recommendations in the QCA's *Non-Statutory National Framework for RE* and can contribute to work on the following themes:

- beliefs and concepts
- ethics and relationships
- rights and responsibilities.

The activities provide experiences and opportunities for discussing, questioning and also responding in a way which offers pupils the chance to use their preferred learning style. Pupils will be able to use a range of forms of expression to communicate their ideas and responses creatively and thoughtfully.

Including every pupil

These four activities aim to get pupils thinking about 'inclusion' for themselves. They reflect the need to set tasks that ask for an individual response dependent on pupil ability. Some of the activities ask pupils to read: some pupils may need additional support in the class or a peer to help them to read. Some of the activities ask pupils to respond in their own chosen way, through a visual or kinaesthetic learning style. One activity asks pupils to respond verbally: there is no pressure to record their views in written form, though a writing frame could be produced to give opportunity for a written response.

I can

I can... The 'I can...' statements reflect the fact that there may be pupils working at many different levels within one class. It's important to think about the levels the pupils are working at, so that tasks can challenge each one, and the learning focus is on developing the skills involved in each level.

Level 1

- Remember and tell someone three things that happened in the story of the Good Samaritan.
- Say how I think people should be treated.

Level 2

- Retell a story of Jesus and say what it might mean to a Christian.
- Respond to a story of kindness with my own opinion.

Level 3

- Describe the importance of religious belief and say how belief can be expressed in the treatment of others.
- Prepare a reflection on the way that we should treat others in society and make a link as to who and what matters to me

Level 4

- Show that I understand how the parable of the Good Samaritan can have an impact on Christians today.
- Describe something which I find spiritual in a story, painting or photograph.

Level 5

- Explain the impact for a Muslim and a Christian of believing that God made human beings all equally valuable.
- Connect my own views about spiritual and religious questions with a point of view I disagree with, explaining in an informed way some difference between tolerance/acceptance.

Activity 1
Image and text

You will need a copy of a story and an accompanying painting. For example, The Story of the Good Samaritan and the painting 'The Good Samaritan' by Vincent Van Gogh (in *Picturing Jesus*, Pack B, RE Today Services). A line drawing is included here. Read the story of the Good Samaritan. It is in Luke ch.10 v.37.

In this story, Jesus told an expert of the law that to inherit eternal life 'you must love your neighbour as yourself'. Think about this for a moment and then complete a response to the words of Jesus using one of the following ideas:

Drawing by
Linda Jeffrey

- Create a sculpture or painting entitled 'Everyone in the World Matters'.

- Compose a reflection on how badly you think some people might be treated around the world.

- Write a modern-day version of the story to express how we should treat others.

- Create a role-play situation where you think about and respond to a scenario of someone being 'excluded' due to their skin colour, size, religion or disability.

- Select a piece of music which you feel has something significant to say about the need to treat everyone equally and with respect. Can you combine this with still images?

Activity 2   Enquiring into a picture

You could use the picture of 'The Good Samaritan' by Vincent Van Gogh (a line drawing is featured, above) as a stimulus for this activity **or** take and then use a digital photograph of something which you find 'inspiring'.

1. This activity draws upon the ideas of a **'community of enquiry'**. Think about the stimulus for a few moments whilst sitting quietly.

2. What question does the picture raise for you?

3. Share your question with three other pupils so you have four questions in your group.

4. Make a decision in the group about which question you like best.

5. One person has to say something about the question.

6. Anyone can then join in by saying 'I agree/disagree because...'.

7. Summarise the points your group have made.

Activity 3   Agree or disagree? A walking discussion activity

Everyone needs a copy of the statements. Walk around the classroom. Get at least 10 other pupils to put their initials onto your sheet to show where their views are. Tell them your views as well.

	1 Strongly agree	2 Agree	3 Not sure	4 Disagree	5 Strongly disagree
1. Everyone is born equal.					
2. No one is better than anyone else.					
3. Your appearance can determine how your life turns out.					
4. Beauty is only skin deep.					
5. Everyone should be treated in the same way.					
6. People with a faith show their care for others more than those without a faith.					
7. I think I am better than others.					
8. We all have a duty to care for our fellow human beings.					
9. Some people have a reason to feel superior to others.					
10. There will always be some people in the world who are 'outcasts'.					

To discuss and write about:

1. What did you find out about the views of others in your class through this activity?

2. Who do you think are the 'outcasts' in our society?

3. How do you think believers of different faiths respond to 'outcasts' in society?

4. Can you think of a religious founder or leader who has worked throughout his or her life to include those others think of as 'outcasts'?

5. Jesus' story of the Good Samaritan is retold hundreds of times every week in school and church. Why?

RE today
Services

Activity 4   The golden rule

Read the following information about 'The Golden Rule'.

The Golden Rule is a moral principle found in virtually all major religions and cultures. It simply means 'treat others as you would like to be treated'.

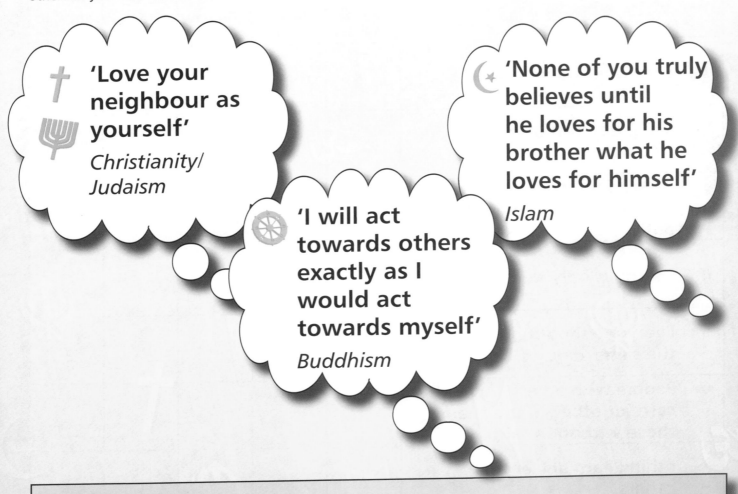

'Love your neighbour as yourself'
Christianity/ Judaism

'I will act towards others exactly as I would act towards myself'
Buddhism

'None of you truly believes until he loves for his brother what he loves for himself'
Islam

To think about/do:

As a class

1. The views above are expressions of belief that those practising Christianity, Judaism, Buddhism and Islam try to follow. Discuss the similarities in the beliefs expressed and whether there are any differences.

2. Quickly jot down what a Humanist would think. Consider what an atheist would think.

In pairs

3. In Hinduism it is important to 'do nothing to others which, if done to you, could cause you pain'.

Discuss how this would work in practice. What difference would it make in our class, school or town if everyone lived by this rule?

On your own

4. Create your own 'Golden Rule'. Discuss with some other learners how to get the wording just right.

5. Make a list of the influences in your life: who has helped you to develop your individual Golden Rule? You could draw a mind map: is it through belief, what your family or friends think, something that has happened in your life that you have come to think in such a way?

6. Imagine you work for an organisation such as the United Nations. You need to encourage a positive way for people to treat others in society. Create a poster containing an image and phrase to share your reflection on 'the way to treat others'.

ICT supporting inclusive practice in RE

For the teacher

In its publication *ICT and Inclusion* (2006), Becta makes the following point about the wide variety of contexts in which the term 'inclusion' is used:

'In all these contexts ICT can support both individuals and groups, and break down some of the barriers that lead to educational exclusion, disaffection and under-achievement. **ICT can be both a medium and a powerful tool in supporting inclusive practice.'**

The following pages look at what happened when ICT was introduced into one RE department that wanted to enhance the exploration of the concept of commitment with Year 8 pupils.

Using digital storytelling, the project involved:

- **engagement, challenge** and **deep learning** for the pupils
- a steep **learning curve** for the teacher
- **contribution** to delivering ICT objectives for the ICT department
- **involvement** of members of the local community
- **digital camera(s)**, some free software and various peripherals.

Why is digital storytelling good for RE?

- It brings the **authentic voice of religion** into the RE classroom: real people, lives and situations.
- It provides **opportunities for dialogue** with people of faith, and encourages respect for all.

What is digital storytelling?

At its simplest, digital storytelling is any narrative which is developed and/or displayed in a digital format. Everyone has a story to tell, and this is one way of exploring, presenting and reflecting on it.

You don't need any special skills to create a digital story – just the story and a digital stills or digital video camera.

Also see

The best way to appreciate what is meant by digital storytelling is to watch some examples!

- **BBC -– Telling Lives**

www.bbc.co.uk/tellinglives

- **Barrie Stephenson (of BBC Telling Lives)**

http://sightings.kidsown.ie/interviews/barrie_stephenson.php.

Acknowledgements: We are grateful to the Year 8 pupils at Archbishop Holgate's School, York, and Head of RE, Olivia Seymour, for sharing the outcomes of their project. Also to the members of Heslington Parish Church for sharing their stories.

The project was funded by DfES/Becta, and was led by RE Today.

REtoday
Services

Digital storytelling

Getting started

Having decided to base the project on digital storytelling, there were several key things which helped to keep the six-lesson project sharply focused on RE from the outset:

- being absolutely clear about the **RE objectives**, and **sharing** them with pupils
- building on the **ICT objectives** for the year group, embedding them in planning and **talking** with the ICT co-ordinator about the implications for the RE
- building on **cross-curricular links**, e.g. literacy
- using a mix of **traditional and ICT-based activities** to introduce the project to pupils (see page 13)
- being **flexible** about how learning objectives were met, e.g. permitting the use of mobile phones and MP3 players
- being **open to learning** from pupils.

ICT links

- **Plan and design** a presentation showing how account has been taken of audience expectations and needs, and the ICT and media facilities available (refining and presenting information).
- **Use ICT effectively** to adapt material for publicaton to wider or remote audiences (communicating).

Literacy links

- **Provide an explanation** or commentary which links words with actions or images (SL4).
- **Listen for and recall** the main points, reflecting on what has been heard, ask searching questions, make comments or challenge the views expressed (SL6).
- **Identify** the underlying themes, implications and issues raised by a talk, reading or programme (SL7).

Expectations: I can ...

Level 4

- **use** religious vocabulary to describe and show understanding of the beliefs and experiences of the religious believer I interview
- **describe** the impact of religion on this person's life
- *raise, and suggest answers to, questions of identity, belonging and commitment.*

Level 5

- **use** a wide religious vocabulary to explain the impact that beliefs have had on the individual I interview
- **explain** why this person belongs to their religion
- *explain answers to questions of identity, belonging and commitment by relating them to my own life and the life of the person I interview.*

Level 6

- **use** religious and philosophical vocabulary to interpret the commitments and beliefs of the person I interview
- **explain** why the impact of religion and belief on the person I interview might vary from another religious believer
- *use reasoning and examples to express insight into the relationship between this person's beliefs and world issues*
- *explain my own and others' views on questions of identity and belonging.*

Introducing commitment

Activity for pupils

Prepare a scrolling presentation of images of people who could be said to be displaying commitment; a good mix of religious and non-religious is needed, such as those shown above. PhotoStory 3, PowerPoint or Clicker are ideal for this purpose.

Ask pupils to:

1. **Look** in silence at the pictures, and **write down** anything that comes to mind as you look at them.

2. **Choose** two pictures that you think have a link. **Describe** the two pictures, and **explain** the link you have made.

3. **Share** your thoughts on the two pictures with a partner. Are there any links between the four pictures you are thinking about? **Explain** any such links.

4. **Suggest** how the pictures you have looked at link with the theme of commitment.

See also

A Google 'image' search is a quick and easy way to find visual stimuli for activities such as the one above. Particularly if this facility is not available in school, why not try one of the following:

• **Flickr**

An online photo management and sharing application:

www.flickr.com

• **Spiritual Photos**

A vast collection of photographs of world religions and spirituality.

www.spiritualphotos.com

Remember to check out the copyright status of any images you plan to use.

To be committed you must stick to what you believe and not give up, no matter what! Committed people are very passionate about what they are committed to; they also try to inspire people around them.

Hannah, Year 8

Some people only say that they are committed, others really are. Whether you are committed to a hobby, a sport or a religion, to be truly committed you must speak up and fight for what you believe in, not just think about it!

Poppy, Year 8

You can show commitment in various ways, e.g. becoming married, helping people in need, fighting in the armed forces, being a leader of a church, working for an emergency service, or protesting for what you believe in.

Arron, Year 8

Commitment is really important for relationships and society as a whole to work well. Without it, it would be harder to trust people, to keep promises and be consistent. Commitment usually involves some sacrifice.

Edward, Year 8

Being inclusive – a checklist for RE with ICT

Effective inclusive teaching occurs when:	Reflections from teachers and pupils
pupils are clear what they will be learning, what they need to do and what the criteria are to judge when the learning has been achieved.	'Pupils were given a lesson-by-lesson outline for the project. This included an introduction to what was expected, assessment criteria, background lessons to introduce the theme and skills for key tasks, e.g. planning questions.'
links are made to learning elsewhere in the curriculum or in intervention groups, helping pupils transfer their knowledge and understanding in different contexts.	'The project was not only planned with the RE learning objectives in mind, it was also planned to build on what pupils had already learned in ICT, or would be learning during that academic year. Apart from being good for RE, this meant it was much easier for the ICT department to provide the support I needed for the project.'
lesson starters and introductory activities create links with prior knowledge and understanding, are active and enjoyable and create success.	'I thought I knew quite a bit about the meaning of commitment at the start of the project, but interviewing Bob helped me not only learn about his faith, but also how it compares to mine, which I found interesting.'
there are frequent opportunities for purposeful talk, for learning through use of talk partners or structured small-group tasks with supportive peers.	'The main thing I learned in RE lessons is that I can work in a group and that we can organise our own work. This way of learning was more interesting.'
pupils are encouraged to ask questions to clarify understanding.	'I learned how to plan and ask good questions, how to ask a follow-on question if I didn't understand or wanted to know more, and how to interpret answers to use in my work.'
pupils have personal targets which they own and are working towards in the lesson.	'We were deciding what we were going to do. We tend to learn more when we are planning our own lessons based on the assessment criteria and personal targets provided by the teacher.'
the teacher models the process, explaining what they are doing, thinking and questioning aloud.	'Pupils needed a variety of skills including using the digital camera for stills and movie, editing and importing photos, etc. The teacher needed to have an understanding of all these skills to model to them how to develop and present their digital stories.'
homework or pre-learning is referred to and used to move pupils forward within the lesson	'Pupils worked in mixed ability groups of three or four. These were chosen mainly on geography to allow pupils the flexibility of working outside lesson time. Progress, questions and ideas for moving forward were shared and talked about in lessons.'
strategies for active engagement through a range of different styles are used at various points throughout lessons.	'We used the digital cameras and went out of school. It was a lot more physical and we could choose and plan our own schedule, and how we learn. I think that it encouraged me to do more work.'
lessons conclude with plenaries that support pupils in reflecting openly on what they've learned and how this fits with what is coming next.	'Pupils fed back to the whole class at regular intervals during the project, reflecting on their own progress, and planning the next steps, as well as encouraging, and learning from, others.'

Source of criteria for an inclusive lesson: *Pedagogy and Practice: Teaching and Learning in Secondary Schools*, Unit 4: Lesson design for Inclusion (DfES 0427 2004 G).

Working with digital images – try these

Idea 1 Using PhotoStory 3

PhotoStory 3 is a free download from Microsoft which provides a stunningly simple way of bringing digital photographs to life – digital storytelling!

Easy and intuitive to use, it is suitable for use by pupils of all ages, 4–19 and beyond. **Within a matter of minutes** (literally) you can be playing a simple slideshow of your own photographs.

Take a little longer, and you can:

- touch, crop or rotate pictures
- add special effects, soundtracks or your own voice, and add titles and captions
- email the slideshow to a friend, watch it on a TV, a computer, or any Windows Mobile-based portable device.

Getting started:

- **Download PhotoStory 3**

www.microsoft.com/windowsxp/ using/digitalphotography/ photostory/default.mspx

- **Find out how to use it – a tutorial from BT**

This site provides an excellent hands-on tutorial that takes you step-by-step through all you need to do to create great digital stories:

www.bteducation.org/img/lib/ dialogics/PhotoMovie/index.html

- **Check out what other people have done**

  - **The nine demos** on this site need Windows XP with Media Player 10.

    www.greece.k12.ny.us/task/ photostory/ps3demos.htm

  - **These demos illustrate the educational use** of digital storytelling.

    www.coe.uh.edu/digital- storytelling/examples.htm

Idea 2 Using the PATHE video archive

It's not always possible to provide your own video footage, but this is no reason why pupils can't work with digital video in RE.

The British PATHE news archive contains over 3,400 hours of film news items covering the years of national and international news from 1901 to 1970. Items useful in RE include footage of Martin Luther King Jnr, Gandhi and the Dalai Lama.

PATHE allows schools **free access** to the high-quality versions of their materials for educational use, which would otherwise cost over £500 each.

See: www.britishpathe.com/index.html

A teacher can:

- **download clips and save** them offline to be shown via a digital projector or whiteboard technologies at the appropriate time during a lesson to illustrate a point or provide stimulus for discussion
- **provide opportunities** for pupils to use presentation software, e.g. Microsoft PowerPoint, to create a professional quality presentation (where pupils are already proficient with the software) to reflect their learning in RE.

Pupils can

- **enrich a presentation** by selecting, downloading and incorporating appropriate video footage from the PATHE archive.

Note

Where the school system does not support users to download files, or where multiple downloads by pupils strains the connection speed, you can arrange for a selection to be downloaded prior to the lesson, and made available locally.

Including gifted pupils in RE

For the teacher

A commitment to inclusion involves meeting the learning needs of all, including the gifted and talented (G&T) pupil in RE. The focus here takes the ideas about 'why people matter' and 'what is the self/what does it mean to be human' from varied religious and atheistic sources for learning about the concept of 'the self': what is 'self'? Should we esteem the self, as the UK culture does? Or deny and sacrifice it as the Christians say? Is the self an illusion, the Buddhists view? Should you submit the self to Allah, with the Muslims?

These pages will exemplify G&T differentiation strategies using Christian, Buddhist and Muslim examples along with some from contemporary secular culture. Page 20 offers some theoretical support to the activities.

Activity 1   What makes a self?

To get pupils thinking about what we mean by 'self', ask them in pairs to complete the image in the next column, for a fictional character, by writing in all the notes and additions they can. Try: Harry Potter, Rachel from Friends, Shrek, Spiderman, Ugly Betty or whoever is current. Can learners guess who the other pairs were thinking of? Then get them to complete a 'self image' for themselves. This can be private if they wish. Discuss the idea that 'self' is hard to define, and that all selves are different.

Six opening questions

- What is the self?
- What is your identity?
- How has it been formed?
- Why do the Buddhists believe there is no self?
- Why do the Christians ask people to sacrifice themselves?
- What does it mean for Muslims to submit the self to Allah?

Make an image of the self

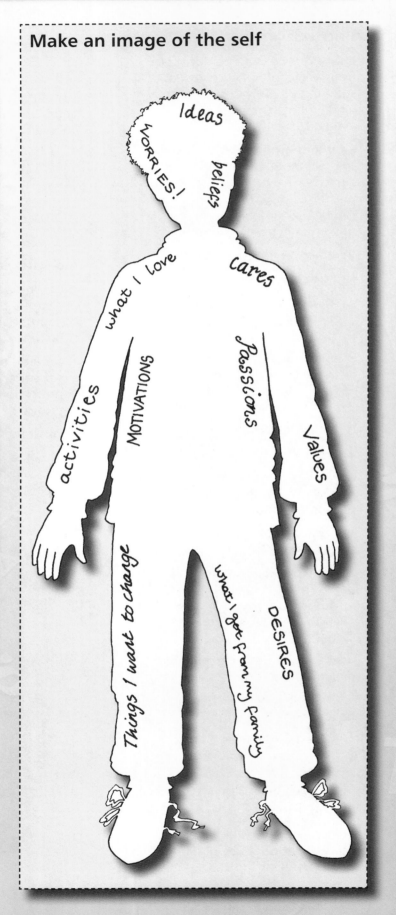

Activity 2   Compare four perspectives on 'the self'

Cut copies of this page into four cards, and make a set for each pair of pupils. Ask them to do three things with the cards:

1. Rank them 1–4 from the one that is closest to their own view to the one furthest from their perspective.

2. Note down three questions that each perspective on 'self' raises for them.

3. Think up two implications of each of these views of the self – how would it lead the Buddhist, Muslim, Christian and Humanist to behave?

'I know a monk who shaves his eyebrows. It's a way of setting aside the vain, clinging craving for physical comfort or good looks. If Paris Hilton is an example of what western society celebrates, then I think that is the opposite of what the Buddha taught. Buddhist teaching is that the self is a kind of illusion, a part of a dream. There is no 'real you', just a collection of distractions picked up along the way through life. We think so much about 'I', 'me' and 'mine' that we are fooled: this 'self' is not real at all. Everything keeps changing, all of us are fluid. There isn't a fixed "self".'

'Christians believe that the "self" or "soul" is the gift of God, but that it's been corrupted by evil or sin. We were made to be friends with God, but our bad actions have broken the friendship. God has given us great gifts – to learn, to laugh, to love, to make music, to create. But we've turned all these gifts as much into evil as into goodness. The corrupted self is all twisted up: it needs to be renewed. We believe that selfishness can be set aside, through the example of Jesus and the power of God's Spirit. Jesus taught us: live a life of love. By his power, we'll win against our own selves.'

'The Muslim tradition says that Allah has given you one life, and the purpose of life is to find Allah, and submit to Him. We are all born as worshippers of Allah, but some of us drift away to selfish ways of life. Anyone can come back to Allah. When we take our final journey – death – then this life and this "self" will seem like a dream to us. The next life, which we hope will be in Paradise, is the real thing. So we use this life as a test bed, a proving ground and a trial run, and we rely on the mercy of Allah so that we will become our true selves in the next life.'

'A Humanist is a person who believes in humanity, but not in gods or angels. Humanist ideas about the self vary. We think that science explains best what it means to be human, so we think we are evolved from other life forms. We like the idea that you can be good without God, and we love the way human ingenuity and inventiveness makes life better. We like the idea that humans can find good reasons to love the truth and love each other without any religion making or forcing them to do it.'

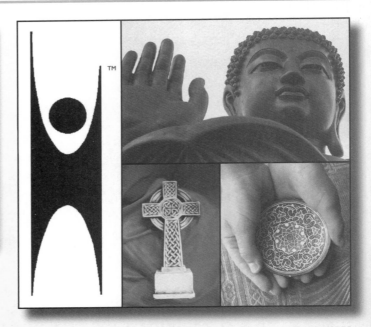

Activity 3 Implications of your view of the self

Here are four more quotations that match the perspectives given on page 17. They show what difference our view of the self might make. Again, cut the cards and give a set to each pair of pupils. Ask them to match the actions to the other sets of cards. The aim of this activity is to generate discussion and ideas about the differences between the views of the self held in various traditions.

'In our tradition, we follow the teaching that a human birth is very precious, because it gives you the chance to seek enlightenment. So the Karuna Trust, a charity working in India, runs education hostels for the poorest people in some Indian villages. We want to act on the feeling of compassion. We want to make suffering less in the world, so we provide education, homes and training for the poorest people of all.'

'God loves everyone equally. All souls are precious. One person I admire deeply is against abortion because of her beliefs – she thinks God gives every life, and all are valuable. Instead of just protesting she issued a call all over India: "If you have a baby, and you don't want the baby, then I want the child. Send the babies to me." She set up the biggest adoption agency in all India.

That sort of action puts our ideas about the self as God's gift into action.'

'One charity that lots of our members support runs computer courses, well-digging projects and educational initiatives, specially for girls in countries like Pakistan, Afghanistan and Bosnia. Our places of worship are open to anyone to come and pray. We also take special care for funeral arrangements, because of what we believe about life after death in Paradise.'

'If you believe in yourself, but not in god or gods, then you can work out for yourself what the good life means. Committing to the truth, accepting life's limitations and trying to live for others as well as yourself is an obvious path. You don't need a visit from an angel to show you this. So look at your history, and into your own mind to find out who you are, then put your energy into living for the good of everyone as far as you can.'

Activity 4   Creative writing: Belief about the self

Ask pupils to choose one of these four 'starts' to write a piece of fiction. Using creative writing often gives a structured starting point, but complete open-endedness, to pupils. It can deploy high-level narrative skills in the service of the exploration of RE's key concepts. Choice helps too. Try it.

I don't believe in submission to anyone really. You have to stand up for yourself, or no one else will. So I find the Muslim idea of submitting to Allah almost an insult. Everyone should stand tall and walk proud! My friend Nassema proved me wrong, though. I was out with her when she was bullied on the bus the other night. I suppose it was racist. I was dead impressed with how she handled it...

John Donne said, over 300 years ago [in *Devotions* XVII], that no one is an island: everyone is a part of the continent. I'm quite an individual person, so when we read his poem in Literature, it made me think whether it's true or not. Then when I got home, I really had to think, because of what had happened to my mum...

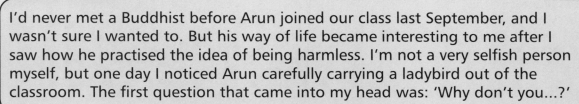

I'd never met a Buddhist before Arun joined our class last September, and I wasn't sure I wanted to. But his way of life became interesting to me after I saw how he practised the idea of being harmless. I'm not a very selfish person myself, but one day I noticed Arun carefully carrying a ladybird out of the classroom. The first question that came into my head was: 'Why don't you...?'

When someone dies, it makes you think: What has happened to them? Where has the person I knew and loved gone now? I've been thinking about this because of my gran's funeral. She was a Christian, and in the funeral they read a line from the Bible that really struck me: 'forever with the Lord'. I walked home from the church, thinking...

Gifted and talented pupils in RE

Ten pointers to plan inclusion for RE

These refer to the previous examples of work about the self, but also apply much more widely to the week-to-week curriculum planning that RE teachers do all the time.

1. Gifted, most able, more able or talented pupils (various terms are in use) are present in every class and every school. It is part of the RE teacher's task to meet their learning needs in personalised ways. These pupils deserve to have their 'special needs' met in RE, with specific RE curricular objectives (just like everyone else).

2. RE talent is not quite the same as general talent: some pupils have particular spiritual insight, or argumentative skill, or deep knowledge of their own faith, so catering for them must be flexible. The work on 'the self' makes space for their own views to be expressed well. RE talents and gifts are best seen as specific to the skills of RE.

3. Gifts and talents in RE come in a variety of shapes, from logical to spiritual, critical to creative. All deserve to be noticed and nurtured. The work on the self includes diverse visual and philosophical ideas, to match a range of talents.

4. Showing an RE talent is often interdependent with language skills – but not always. RE uses the language skills pupils have, but also offers chances to show insight without writing.

5. 'The task's the thing': setting tasks with a high ceiling or no ceiling at all is good for G&T pupils in RE. Contemplation of the nature of the self is at the heart of this work: nothing easy about that.

6. QCA Levels 6, 7, 8 and EP are a good tool for RE professionals in setting good 'top end' tasks. In this work, the potential is to interpret diverse religious ideas about the self (L6), evaluate different ideas about the self using philosophical concepts (L7) and synthesise ideas from psychology and religion about the self (L8).

7. Good practice for G&T pupils often implies good RE for pupils of all abilities. The work about the self is open to a lower achiever, at least in Activities 1 and 2. Sometimes the learning needs of G&T pupils require quite specific planning and learning activities.

8. Evidence of achievement may be spoken, creative, dramatic, written – a balance is desirable. In this work, the talk and listen parts are as important as the read and write parts.

9. Teaching gifted and talented pupils: can we make it a pleasure, or will it remain a problem? The activities on pages 16–19 offer one simple way of getting the G&T pupils motivated, and using interesting models and examples from their work for the whole class.

10. If a syllabus writer required 12-year-olds to analyse the relative merits of different conceptions of the self in a range of religions, teacher might ask 'Who writes this stuff? How are we supposed to do this?' But if some pupils can do the activities on pages 16–19, then shouldn't they be given the chance to do so? Inclusive RE says 'Yes' to that.

There is a selection of additional materials to help teaching the gifted and talented on the RE Today website. www.retoday.org.uk/downloads.htm#gt

Including the religious margin: Druidry, Jehovah's Witnesses and the Baha'i faith

For the teacher

These materials help pupils to explore faiths that are not usually studied in RE, even though they are present in the UK and internationally and may be active in the local community. Some pupils may have personal or family links to these faiths. Other pupils may be in total ignorance, curious, misinformed or hostile. These materials recognise and value religious diversity by presenting distinctive perspectives on religious and moral questions, helping pupils to develop skills in analysis, evaluation and reflection, particularly on questions like:

- What is God/Spirit like?
- How does God reveal himself/herself/itself?
- What or who should have authority in life?
- How should we deal with the plurality of religions and claims to truth?
- How do particular beliefs affect people's moral behaviour and contribution to society?

Key terms and concepts

These faiths are useful in raising and answering questions about these terms:

theism, pantheism, animism, trinity, transcendence, immanence, manifestation, creed, revelation, progressive revelation, inter-faith dialogue

Key moral and social issues

These faiths are particularly useful in raising and answering questions about:

- Medical ethics/science and religion; life and death rights and responsibilities regarding giving and receiving of blood; alternative and complementary approaches to health care
- Religious persecution
- Environmental issues
- Social harmony.

Links to English RE's Non-Statutory National Framework

Breath of study: through learning about a religious community with a significant local presence.

Themes: beliefs and concepts, authority, moral choices, responsibilities, global issues and inter-faith dialogue.

Attitudes: open-mindedness; respect for all.

Supporting citizenship education: diversity of national, regional, religious identities and need for mutual respect and understanding, debating topical spiritual, moral and cultural issues.

Possible learning objectives

This work aims to enable pupils to:

- become familiar with some non-traditional belief systems
- evaluate how beliefs influence and affect actions and commitments
- analyse similarities and differences between faiths/belief systems
- eradicate prejudicial thinking and promote a critical but positive understanding of beliefs and actions which may be different to one's own
- reflect on these religious perspectives and on their own beliefs.

Possible learning outcomes

I can...

Level 3
- describe some minority religious beliefs and show how these affect people's actions;
- describe what I believe is important and how this affects my behaviour.

Level 4
- use religious vocabulary to show I understand how beliefs affect people's actions;
- apply the idea of 'the influence of belief' to me and my behaviour.

Level 5
- use religious vocabulary to explain distinctive aspects of beliefs as well as similarities and explain how these affect actions;
- explain the challenge of putting belief into practice, for me and for others.

Level 6
- use religious vocabulary to interpret a wide range of distinctive beliefs and actions;
- express my insights into the challenge to beliefs and commitments presented by some moral or global issues.

Four learning activities

Copy pages 22 and 23 for pupils. There are three statements, from a Druid, a Baha'i and a Jehovah's Witness, to read. The 16 statements at the end of page 23 can be used for the four activities described on pages 24 and 25.

You may also like to make sets of the 16 statements, enlarged and cut up on card. The activities are easier to run if you have a set of these cards for each group of 3–6 pupils.

We think it's important to support the environment. We get involved in green issues, recycling and so on.	We have no creed or formal organisation, so we rely on ourselves to make our own decisions.	We believe God is in and not separate from all of Nature. So we treat all life with great respect.	We do not believe human beings are superior to animals. So, often, we are vegetarian.
We believe in the Bible and Jesus Christ, but not in the doctrine of the Trinity, so we often disagree with other Christians' interpretation of the Bible.	We only obey our country's laws if they are not in conflict with God's laws, so sometimes we have to go against the flow.	We believe the Bible is the full guide to truth and all aspects of morality, so we spend a great deal of time studying it and learning passages by heart.	We don't have any rules, but one of our sayings is 'do what you like as long as you hurt no one'. So all acts which don't hurt others are considered moral.
We do not believe in fighting: so if there was a war we would be conscientious objectors.	We believe that our religion is true and all others are misguided. So we think it is our duty to teach others about the truth.	We believe that God reveals himself through different messengers – Krishna, Buddha, Jesus, Muhammad (pbuh) and our own prophet, Bahá'u'lláh. So we show respect to them all.	We believe that religion is the greatest way to bring about peace, order and contentment in the world. So we support the study and understanding of religion as much as we can.
There is great diversity of practice. Some people prefer a practical experience of nature, others prefer studying by themselves.	We believe that God's truth can be found in all religions. So we are happy to learn about and work with other religions.	We believe religion and human civilisation is always progressing. So we are always hopeful and optimistic in our outlook.	We believe in the unity of all people. So we often get very involved in inter-faith and intercultural events.

I'm Peter, and I'm a Jehovah's Witness. We are dedicated to God. We bear witness concerning Jehovah, the personal name for God (Isaiah ch.43, vs10; Psalm 83, vs18). God is love and he loves his people. We believe that during the reign of God's Kingdom (the theme of Jesus ministry) human beings who are dead will rise again (they had been asleep). Human beings who exercise faith in God will live for ever as subjects of God's Kingdom on a cleansed earth (Rev. ch.21, vs3, 4). There is no idea of hell. Those who do not exercise faith will remain dead (Romans ch.6, vs23). God's Kingdom is a heavenly government ruled by Christ Jesus and 144,000 co-rulers taken from the earth (Rev. ch.5, vs9, 10; ch.14, vs1). In the Bible it says that Christians should 'abstain from blood' (Gen. ch.9, vs3, 4; Lev. ch.17, vs14; Acts ch.15, vs 28, 29); therefore we refuse to eat blood or have blood transfusions. I carry a medical card which states my wish not to have a blood transfusion.

We don't celebrate Christmas, Easter or birthdays. The only celebration Jesus gave instructions for was to memorialise his death (Luke ch.22, vs19). We also believe that many of the customs associated with Christmas and Easter were originally pagan in origin and therefore are contaminated and unChristian. We believe the principal key to identifying true religion is love (John ch.13, vs35). Although Christian-based, Jehovah's Witnesses believe that the traditional Christian Churches have moved away from the true teachings of the Bible, and do not work in full harmony with God. Many of the traditional Christian Churches do not think Jehovah's Witnesses are a mainstream Christian denomination because we reject the Christian doctrine of the Trinity, which we regard as both irrational and unbiblical.

Taken from http://www.bbc.co.uk/religion /religions/witnesses

I'm Jean, and I belong to the Baha'i faith. I was brought up as a Church of England Christian but when I was 13 my parents became Baha'i and I followed. As a young adult I went to Pakistan, to join my Iraqi husband (also a Baha'i) who was studying there. There is an expectation for Baha'i people to know about all faiths: we look for the similarities and also see the differences. We think the distinctiveness of each religion is a result of them springing from different times and places, but there are significant similarities such as the message of love, the need for honesty, truthfulness and purity.

I take my turn in hosting Baha'i meetings in my house. We read from Baha'u'llah's words. We don't have any clergy: rather there is a local spiritual assembly elected every year. I am active in the Lancashire Forum of Faiths. We promote intercultural and inter-faith activities such as information meetings about each other's faiths. We are recognised as one of the nine faiths in the UK's Interfaith Network. As a Baha'i, my aim is to bring about world unity.

Baha'is have often been persecuted for their faith. Some 'born-again' Christians think we will go to hell and some Muslims believe we will not enter paradise. In Iran Baha'i are not allowed to be educated. In Egypt in December 2006 human rights organisations became involved in cases where Baha'i were persecuted. Because of our peaceful nature and our belief in world unity, a Baha'i is often chosen to be the spokesperson in inter-faith debates worldwide. We are recognised as being an inclusive faith.

I'm Heather. I am a Druid. Most Druids are pagans: that's the umbrella term. Druidry is more like a philosophy or a way of life than a religion as such. We are all spirits, fragments of God. Some people follow Druidism as a belief system in its own right but Druidism is open to those of all faiths or none. Some people describe themselves as a Bu ddhist Druid, a Christian Druid or atheist Druid because they prefer a 'stance' which has no creed or formal organisation. One of my friends is a Christian Druid: she goes to church but she also comes to Druid celebrations with me and she has a real love of nature.

Most of us believe in the spiritual nature of life and many of us are **pantheist** or **animist**. This means believing that there is no personal god but rather god is in everything. So we don't really see god as transcendent but rather manifest *in* everything. Many Druids believe in an afterlife, but we focus more on this life and how we can contribute to the preservation and evolution of the natural world and fulfil our own potential creativity. We have a love of trees and stones, animals and human beings. We believe in the power of dreams and many Druids consider that the subconscious communicates through dreams. The subconscious doesn't have words so it speaks to us through dreams.

WE celebrate seasonal festivals including the two solstices and two equinoxes. We gather together in great numbers at sites such as Stonehenge, but some Druids celebrate on their own, meditating. I usually participate in the seasonal celebrations – I'm off on a retreat to celebrate Imbolc next week. Many Druids believe in holistic medicine: treating the whole person not just the individual symptom. Some of us prefer to use complementary medicine. But we often combine conventional medicine with alternative remedies because I think it would be stupid to ignore the advances of science. We don't try to convert people: follow Druidry if you feel it's right for you. We believe in personal freedom.

Four suggested activities

Activity 1   Washing line

The 16 statements from page 22 are all about the impact of beliefs: 'We believe ... so what we do is...' Taking each statement one by one, some or all of the pupils arrange themselves along a continuum line (washing line) from 'Strongly Agree' to 'Strongly Disagree'. Alternatively they may write their names on a card and place them on an actual washing line, responding to some or all of the 16 statements, or use Blu-Tack ® to place them along a 'wall continuum'. Discussion and comment should focus on giving reasons and linking to experience.

Activity 2   Target practice

Using cut-outs from the statement bank from page 22, each pupil categorises some statements onto the target, representing their own opinions. Done in groups of four, with time to explain their points of view, this is a good way of encouraging purposeful speaking and listening in RE. An interactive whiteboard would be a helpful way to take feedback from the class: pupils could drag and drop each statement into the required position.

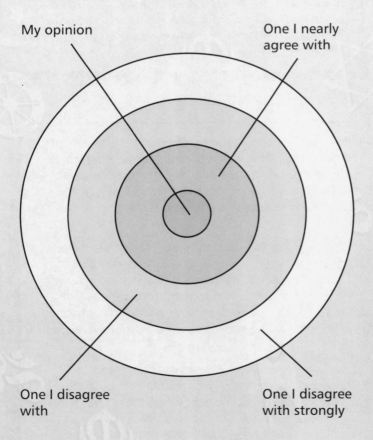

My opinion

One I nearly agree with

One I disagree with

One I disagree with strongly

Activity 3   Blood transfusions

In groups, pupils prepare a short presentation for a debate about blood transfusions:

- explain **why** Jehovah's witnesses **refuse blood transfusions**;
- describe how some doctors have started to **use bloodless surgery**;
- conclude your presentation by explaining **what you have learnt** and **what you think about Jehovah's Witnesses' beliefs** and the **medical responses** to them.

Some students could debate FOR blood transfusions (including doctors) – others can take the Jehovah's Witness side and argue AGAINST blood transfusions (including doctors).

http://www.watchtower.org/library/g/2003/12/8/article_01.htm

– an article from *Watchtower* 'I accepted God's view of blood'. This article is a description of a young doctor's conversion to Jehovah's Witnesses and his understanding of the teaching about not taking blood into the body. Follow the links to the Jehovah's Witness Bible references.

http://www.watchtower.org/e/vcnb/article_01.htm – a short video which outlines how some medical professionals have risen to the challenge of developing techniques which avoid using blood transfusions.

http://www.watchtower.org/e/hb/index.htm?article=article_03.htm – blood transfusions – other options.

Activity 4   Thinking hats

This activity asks pupils to work in a group of six and take one style of thinking to be the basis for their contribution. Enlarge the framework on page 25, and put the 16 statements face down in the centre. When each statement is turned up, the six people make comments from the point of view of the 'hat' they have been given to wear. This aims to provide focused, rounded and diverse discussion. It's a powerful method of problem analysis.

Edward De Bono's six hats

Red Hat (focus on your gut reactions and emotions)

Something I like about this is ... Something I dislike about this is ...

My first feeling/gut reaction/instinct about this is ...

The way I think different people will feel about this is ...

Yellow Hat (positive and optimistic)

One thing I think that's good about this is ...

One useful thing about this is ...

One way this benefits people is that ...

White Hat (focus on data)

Explaining this in my own words I think this means ...

Blue Hat (controls and plans)

The parts of this statement we completed well/ struggled with were ...

This card has been useful to help me think about ...

This card makes me think that it would be useful to find out more about ...

CARD

Black Hat (cautious and defensive)

One problem/difficulty/ danger of this is ...

This doesn't make sense because ...

Green Hat (creative and imaginative)

One thing that is interesting about this is ...

This gives me a new idea/ way of thinking about ...

On the RE Today website:

Additional guidance, materials and ideas for using this topic can be found on the members area of the RE Today website, including a PowerPoint presentation to introduce the 'Six Hats' activity to pupils. See this term's *REtoday* magazine for the members' password.

On Druidry

P. Carr-Gomm, *What do Druids Believe?* London: Granta Publications, 2006.
http://www.druidry.org/ – Introduction to Druidry
http://www.bbc.co.uk/religion/religions/paganism/holydays/year.shtml – Festivals in paganism
http://www.tylwythteg.com/druid1.html – Interesting site
www.paganfed.org.uk – About generic Paganism

On Jehovah's Witnesses

http://www.bbc.co.uk/religion/religions/witnesses/ – General introduction to Jehovah's Witnesses
http://www.bbc.co.uk/religion/religions/witnesses/beliefs/beliefs.shtml – beliefs
Jehovah's Witnesses: Who Are They and What Do They Believe? London: Watchtower Bible and Tract Society of Britain, 2000.
Mankind's Search for God, New York: Watchtower Bible and Tract Society of New York, 1990.
www.natre.org.uk – Free download of James Holt's article on 'Jehovah's Witnesses in the RE Classroom' from *REsource*, Spring 2007.

On the Baha'i Faith

All Religions are One, Spiritual Assembly of the Baha'i, Baha'i of Warwick (n.d.).
Bahá'u'lláh cited in *The Promise of World Peace*, Statement by the Universal House of Justice, Baha'i World Centre, Haifa.
http://www.bbc.co.uk/religion/religions/bahai/ – Excellent resource for all areas of Baha'i faith
http://www.bahai.org.uk/gi/intro.htm – General introduction
http://www.bahai.org.uk/bhw/1.htm and http://www.bbc.co.uk/religion/religions/bahai/customs/prayer_1.shtml – About prayer.

RE against racism

Teacher's notes

RE provides opportunities to explore prejudice in a safe environment: we all hold prejudices, sometimes without realising it. The danger is when prejudice turns into discrimination or racism, purposefully or unwittingly. The approaches covered in these pages encourage students in the 13–16 age range to relate their learning in RE to their own attitudes. Initial activities encourage students to learn more about each other (especially those they would not usually mix with), to encourage mutual respect for those who are not like them. This prepares them for critical analysis of issues such as prejudice, discrimination, stereotyping, bias and racism. Students can then develop their understanding of the value of dialogue to gain a greater understanding of how religion and belief contribute to community cohesion. The work aims to recognise the various perceptions people have regarding the roles of religion in the world (see QCA's *Non-Statutory National Framework*, p.30).

The RE work has links to Citizenship: exploring the implications of the diverse national, regional, religious and ethnic identities in UK and the need for mutual respect and understanding (QCA, *Citizenship*, p.15).

GCSE skills

* recall, select, organise and deploy knowledge of the specification content about race and prejudice;

* describe, analyse and explain the relevance and application of religious ideas about racism;

* evaluate different responses to religious and moral issues, using relevant evidence and argument.

'I can ...' statements

Level 6

* interpret religious ideas about questions of race, identity and commitment for myself in the light of religious teaching.

Level 7

* use some of the methods of religious study to evaluate issues about racism, identity and commitment for myself, employing a wide philosophical and religious vocabulary.

Resources

http://www.100greatblackbritons.com/list.html

http://www.cre.gov.uk/index.html

Wilberforce's Christian faith prompted social reform:

http://www.bbc.co.uk/history/historic_figures/wilberforce_william.shtml

The Interfaith Network – http://www.interfaith.org.uk/

Activity 1   Seeing people as individuals

Key terms: prejudice, discrimination, racism, institutional racism, bias, stereotype, segregation, integration.

Task 1: How well do we know each other?

Make a set of 30 words on cards, each one describing a personal quality. Pupils work in groups of four or five. Pick up a card and give it to the person in the group that card best describes (T. Bond, *180 Games for Social Life Skills*, London: Hutchinson, 1986).

Task 2: Who am I?

Pupils write down on a piece of paper one thing about themselves that the class would probably not expect, which will surprise or amaze the class. Collect the paper slips and read out one at a time. Pupils write down who they think the person is. How many did they get? Any big surprises? Variation: as homework, ask students to bring a surprising fact about a family member.

Task 3: How do we react to people?

Each person wears a headband 'identity' on their heads. Pupils do not know what is written on their forehead. The task is for the whole group to mill around, talk to each other and arrange a class weekend camp together: Where to go? What to do? How to arrange the trip? They are to react to everyone according to the label on their head, never saying what the label is. *Variation:* they can mill around but not speak – simply react to each others' labels non-verbally.

After 5–6 minutes stop the activity and ask them:

• What do you think your label said?

• How do you know?

• Did it affect the way people reacted to you?

Examples: Bad tempered, very funny person, bully, depressed, friendly, leader, shy, caring person, good at sport, practical joker, reliable, boring, liar, good at solving problems, practical, imaginative, double-crosser,

Debrief: What kind of people do people like or not like? What does this activity tell us about prejudice and stereotypes? (Bond, *180 Games for Social Life Skills*, p.149)

Task 4: Anti-racist posters: What works? Evaluate the mission of the Commission for Equality and Human Rights (CEHR, formerly the Commission for Race Equality). Look at the four anti-racist posters from CEHR – http://www.cre.gov.uk/publs/cat_posters.html

What messages are CEHR trying to communicate? Do religious teachings support each of these messages? Which is the most effective poster/teaching? Why?

Task 5: Seeing things from the opposite viewpoint

Work with this extract from Malorie Blackman, *Noughts & Crosses* (London: Corgi Books, 2002), pp.37-38.

[Mum, Dad and son (Callum) are all noughts (white people). Callum has been selected as one of the first noughts to be taught at Heathcroft School – previously made up of crosses (black people). Noughts are the underclass.]

• 'Religion is part of the problem of a divided society, not the solution.' Do you agree?

• What are the advantages/disadvantages/consequences of segregation/integration?

• Do you think that it's a good idea to try to make schools take pupils from different backgrounds to balance the ethnic, cultural and religious mix?

'I still think he's making a big mistake …' Mum sniffed.

'Well, I don't.' Dad's smile vanished as he turned to Mum.

'He doesn't need to go to their schools. We Noughts should have our own schools with the same opportunities that the Crosses enjoy,' Mum retorted. 'We don't need to mix with them.'

'What's wrong with mixing?' I asked, surprised.

'It doesn't work,' Mum replied at once. 'As long as the schools are run by Crosses, we'll always be treated as second-class, second-best nothings. We should look after and educate our own, not wait for the Crosses to do it for us.'

'You never used to believe that,' said Dad.

'I'm not as naive as I used to be – if that's what you mean.' Mum replied.

I opened my mouth to speak but the words wouldn't come. They were just a jumble in my head. If a Cross had said that to me, I'd be accusing them of all sorts. It seemed to me we'd practised segregation for centuries now and that hadn't worked either. What would satisfy all the Noughts and the Crosses who felt the same as Mum? Separate countries? Separate planets? How far away was far enough? What was it about the differences in others that scared some people so much?

From *Noughts and Crosses* by Malorie Blackman (Corgi Children's Books, 2006) used with permission.

Activity 2 John Sentamu and the CEHR

Aim: To reflect on the contribution of individuals and groups who have helped to promote racial harmony. Show pupils these two quotations from the Bible and the Qur'an:

> **Quote 1**: 'From one man God made every nation of men, that they should inhabit the whole earth; and he determined the times set for them and the exact places where they should live. God did this so that men would seek him and perhaps reach out for him and find him, though he is not far from each one of us.'
>
> *Acts ch.17, vs26, 27*

> **Quote 2**: 'O mankind! We have created you from a male and a female, and made you into nations and tribes, that you may know one another. Verily, the most honourable of you with Allâh is that (believer) who is pious. Surely, Allâh is All-Knowing, All-Aware.'
>
> *Qur'an 49:1313*

John Sentamu: First black archbishop for the Church of England

The Church of England appointed the first black archbishop in 2005. John Sentamu is proud of his African roots and works for racial harmony. He was asked to contribute as an adviser in the Stephen Lawrence inquiry which found the police force to be institutionally racist (Macpherson Report, 1999). Sentamu is not afraid to speak out about education:

> **Quote 3**: 'Education is still very Anglo-Saxon in its approach. These failures are not because teachers are racist. They are because the education system has not sufficiently recognised that it's dealing with a multi-ethnic, multicultural society.'
>
> *Archbishop Sentamu*

When he was appointed Archbishop of York, John Sentamu received large amounts of racist hate mail.

Some people sent him excrement through the post.

The archbishop believes in forgiveness. He also disagreed with Trevor Phillips, head of the CEHR, who said that members of the BNP should be refused holy communion in church:

> **Quote 4**: 'Of course the BNP is wrong in its message of ethnic superiority and hatred towards all Muslims, Jews and the rest of us whom it would deport given the first opportunity, but Jesus Christ died for them as well. The communion table must always be open to those who are unworthy of it, and I count myself most unworthy of all to approach the altar of God.'
>
> *Archbishop Sentamu*
>
> http://news.bbc.co.uk/1/hi/england/north_yorkshire/6282665.stm

Discussion in threes or fours:

- Analyse your curriculum: have you learned enough from varied faiths, cultures and races?

- Can you interpret Quotes 1 and 2? Are the Muslim and Christian scriptures anti-racist?

- Do you agree with Quote 3, Sentamu's analysis of the education system? Have you been prepared for life in a multi-ethnic, multicultural society?

- What particular contribution has religion and/or religious education played in this? What else could or should be done?

- Why might it be hard for a black priest to give communion to a BNP supporter?

- What do you think of Sentamu's idea about giving communion to the BNP? (Quote 4)

John Sentamu, Archbishop of York
Photo © Martin Sheppard/Diocese of York

God: father, mother, neither or both?

For the teacher

Most studies of gender differences, both sociological and psychological, have indicated that these differences impact upon both learning styles and interest. Boys tend to do well at clear-cut questions which do not require lengthy explanation. Girls may demonstrate a much better understanding of language.

There are longstanding gender differences in religion. Men are known to be less religious than women. Boys are less likely to choose RE as a subject option. In 2006, 90,000 girls took GCSE RS full courses, but only 69,000 boys. There is also a gender difference which exists within the male-centred religions.

I can ...

Level 3

- Describe beliefs about the main characteristics of God;

- *Make links between ideas of God as either father or mother and my own ideas.*

Level 4

- Show that I understand that in religions God is given human characteristics which symbolise something, and this is often male centred;

- *Apply my own ideas of God's characteristics to how Hindus and Christians see God.*

Level 5

- Analyse the imagery of God in terms of gender and show their effectiveness;

- *Explain my own views about God and gender.*

For information

- In Sikhism, Judaism and Islam, God is believed to be sexless (or gender neutral), but in English, it is improper to speak of a person as 'it'. God has therefore been traditionally referred to as 'He'.

- Giving God human characteristics is called 'anthropomorphism'. Since people are physical beings they are limited in understanding, and so anthropomorphism can help us to relate to and understand more about the idea of God.

- Hindus believe that there is only one ultimate reality, Brahman, who created everything and is everything. The different gods and goddesses are all aspects of Brahman. This Supreme Reality (Brahman) can be seen in both male and female forms. Each of the major gods has a goddess counterpart (or consort), and many Hindus worship the Great Goddess exclusively.

- In Hinduism, Devi is the Divine Mother. The word means 'to shine'. She is the Shining One, the 'Mother Goddess', who is the mother of all and is given different names in different places and in different appearances. As the mother of all life, she is gentle, the goddess of nature and life, bringing rain and protecting against disease. As mother of death, she is terrible.

- The word for 'goddess' in Hinduism is Shakti, which means 'power' or 'energy'. Hindu teaching is that the goddess Shakti is the power and energy with which the universe is created, preserved, destroyed and recreated. She is the driving force behind the whole of creation. Kali is the fearful and ferocious form of the mother goddess.

Thinking about the image of Kali

5. Should we say 'he' or 'she' for God? We think...

6. Hindu iconography shows the destructive and frightening experiences of life as part of the Divine. We think...

4. In Hindu tradition, statues of the goddess Kali show her...

7. From looking at this image, we have learned...

© ArkReligion/Alamy

3. The feelings and emotions associated with the picture might be...

1. Five things we notice about the picture are...

2. Our guesses about the meaning of the picture are...

Work with a partner and complete the first three boxes in as much detail as you can. Then read some more about Kali, and complete the next four boxes.

© Topfoto

Christian images of God

Although most monotheists (believers in one God) think that God is a spirit, and therefore does not have a gender, in Christianity God is usually given a masculine gender. God is generally referred to as 'He'.

There are a few images of God in the Bible which speak of God in female terms but most of the time God is described by male images. He is also frequently called 'Father'. To Christians, God has a relationship to people which is like a good father to children.

Jesus speaks of God the father on many occasions and even uses the term 'Abba', which means daddy.

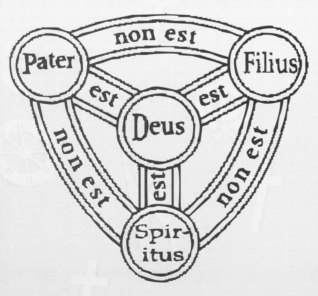

To think about:

- What makes the image of God as a father a good one?
- Why may this not be the case for some people?

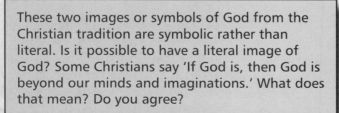

These two images or symbols of God from the Christian tradition are symbolic rather than literal. Is it possible to have a literal image of God? Some Christians say 'If God is, then God is beyond our minds and imaginations.' What does that mean? Do you agree?

Activity 1

Each pupil takes three pieces/strips of paper. Think of three words to describe God. They may refer to God's characteristics.

- **Write** these words on the three pieces of paper. These are then handed to the teacher.

- **In groups, pupils** are given out a selection of the words and asked to sort them into male, female or neutral aspects of God. Are there many female ones? If not, why not?

- **Class debate**: Divide the class into two teams. One team is given the motion: 'God is male', and the other against: 'God is not male'. Give pupils time to prepare. Hear three short speeches on both sides, then let the argument roll.

Activity 2 Father God, mother God

Write a modern-day version of the Lord's Prayer in a female version – 'Our Mother' prayer

Activity 3 Using the picture of Kali

- **In a shower of thought,** write down as many things as you can that strike you about the picture.

- Use the scaffolding table below to write about the female goddess.

Kali's attributes	Description	I think this represents/ says about God
Colour		
Arms		
Face		
Position		

Resources

- www.natre.org.uk/pdfs/resource/25_1_1 will take you to a research report on boy's achievement in RE.

- http://www.cleo.net.uk – Interactive website for pupils. Look at 'Gujurati Hindu Temple' which includes excellent versions of stories of Kali and Durga.

- http://www.exoticindiaart.com/kali.htm – Article for teachers and useful images of female deities and explanation of symbolism.

- http://www.edwinasandys.com is the site of Edwina Sandys, sculptor, and refers interestingly to her 'Christa'.

Ideas for adapting this work

For a more boy-centred interactive or kinaesthetic approach, stations could be used in the room marked either 'male' or 'female' and pupils get up and place the comments in the right area. Or the teacher calls out comments and pupils go to the area where they think the comment belongs.